ALISON BRITTON

PUBLISHED IN THE SAME SERIES

Elizabeth Fritsch In Studio
A view by Peter Dormer and David Cripps

ALISON BRITTON

A VIEW BY PETER DORMER AND DAVID CRIPPS

BELLEW · LONDON

Published by Bellew Publishing Company Ltd
7 Southampton Place
London WC1A 2DR

Text © 1985 Peter Dormer
Photographs © 1985 David Cripps
Illustrations © 1985 John Morgan

First published 1985

ISBN 0 947792 05 8

Printed in Great Britain

CONTENTS

Portrait of
Alison Britton

INTRODUCTION

Alison Britton's viewpoint is, essentially, that: 'Craft is a means
to an end and is not really anything in itself. It consists of doing
something properly, and it is a basis of recognition of values and
skills and methods and knowledge of materials. It has no real
substance or meaning without leaning towards art or design:
the design world and the art world have equal need of it. Craft
is a substratum and not an entity.'[1]

Alison Britton builds pots and she also writes about the
applied arts. In both these roles she can see, looking back over

the last ten years, that the chief impetus of the craft world in the United Kingdom (and it is true, too, of the United States of America) has tended towards art. Now, in the 1980s, there is a strong desire to push crafts towards design.

Britton is right to regard craft as a substratum, but, at the same time, craft and the applied arts occupy a middle ground that is not to be identified with product design and factory production on the one hand or painting and sculpture on the other. The term 'applied arts' is helpful here: an applied artist can, when he wants, ease up on the rigours of functional design in order to indulge his still-utilitarian wares with fancy. The applied artist can flout rules of design because he knows that his useful object has an additional function – decoration. Alternatively, the craftsman who is leaning towards art does not want to be judged alongside fine art. A craftsman's ornament and decoration may be pleasurable, pretty, humorous; and these same adjectives may be applied just as appropriately to a Vermeer or a Donatello. However, in the craftsman's case, those adjectives are all that can be applied and all that he expects to be applied, whereas in the case of the Vermeer or the Donatello they are only a beginning.

The role of the studio potter at this point in the twentieth century allows the potter to be capricious. Even when we expect the potter to provide us with wares that are useful we also expect decoration and ornament. Alison Britton, however, does not make useful wares, she is an ornamentalist.

Britton is one of a generation of English women potters to emerge from the Royal College of Art, London, in the early 1970s. Although they have been presented as a group, Alison Britton's peers, such as Elizabeth Fritsch, Jacqui Poncelet and Jill Crowley, are quite different from one another. What makes them appear to be a group is their success in establishing a new set of directions for English studio pottery. In the 1950s and 1960s there were potters in England trying to establish new directions and do work that was not predominantly brown, clumsy and round, but they did not become well known. (The exceptions are Hans Coper and Lucie Rie.)

These women have talent; they also had luck. The British government, which had already funded fine art and design, started subsidizing the crafts and this made it possible to establish professional exhibitions and good catalogues. An important magazine, *Crafts*, was started, and this became a key vehicle for publicity and promotion, which previous generations of studio potters lacked.

Nevertheless, this RCA 'group' was different in its professionalism and questioning of received values from that of earlier generations of studio potters in the United Kingdom. Britton defines it: 'What sets my generation apart is that we have taken up the borderlines between function and ornament as an area of pursuable interest and excitement.' The orthodoxy had been that there was no beauty without utility – a very English, protestant philosophy which many craftsmen realized had become debilitating.

When Alison Britton left the Royal College in 1973 she worked on several commissions using tiles. Tiles were followed by 'jugs', and currently she makes 'containers', which are asymmetrical, abstract ornamental pots. Throughout each of these stages she has shown a deep interest in decorating the surface of her work, partly a reflection of her enjoyment in experimenting with two-dimensional decoration. Her first art school studies at Leeds College of Art were biased towards drawing and, although she concentrated on pottery techniques and skills at the Central School of Art and Design (London), by the time she got to the Royal College she wanted to do more two-dimensional work. She experimented with photography, but eventually found pottery again by producing tiles. And tiles were attractive because she could draw on them.

When she was a child her parents encouraged her to draw in a free and expressive as well as an analytical manner. This predilection for expressive, gestural line has stayed with Britton and, as we will see, determines her method of working.

Britton comes from a middle-class intellectual and artistic family, and this is important in that studio pottery in England is a middle-class interest and occupation. Its roots are recent and owe a lot to Bernard Leach, a middle-class individual who 'rebelled' by putting his hands in the mud. Before the First World War studio pottery in Europe was produced by gentlemen potters, who let others do the rough work of making the pots and kept themselves clean for the noble task of decoration. But, in taking over the craft of pottery, the middle classes, both makers and purchasers, naturally transformed it into a reflective, self-conscious activity. One of the reasons why studio pottery took off as an honourable and worthwhile (if poorly remunerated) activity in England in the 1920s and 1930s was because Bernard Leach was so articulate. He could argue his way through to new reasons for making pots and articulate a defence for making only marginally useful wares. Of course, the gain for pottery was and is that the craft is still alive and vital when commonsense would have prophesied its demise.

Britton shares with Leach an ability to write and she warms to people who are both literate and visually aware – a duality she expresses by being both a potter and a writer about pots. But why make pots? 'I like clay, it is wet, sticky, and versatile – you can make anything from figurines to sanitary ware.'

Britton's first solo exhibition was at the Amalgam Gallery, London, in 1976, and her reputation as a studio potter was consolidated at the Crafts Council's Gallery in 1979, which showed an astonishing collection of jugs, which, once and for all, demonstrated that she was a master of the art of achieving congruity between form and its decoration. The indecision that had earlier resulted in her keeping to decoration on tiles rather than making full-blown three-dimensional pots had been set aside during the years 1976 to 1979. She had succeeded in thinking her way through to combining her interest in drawing with her desire for three-dimensional form.

ASYMMETRY
AND THE DISSEMBLING JUG

Although Alison Britton learned to throw at the wheel when she was a student, she says, 'I don't like round things, I like asymmetry – after all, I'm asymmetrical myself as indeed we all are!' She understands, however, the appeal that traditional pots have for some people: 'For some, part of the satisfaction in looking at and feeling a thrown pot is in its rotundity, its unchangingness as it is spun round; the glaze may vary from place to place, which is exciting in the regular context of the unity and wholeness of a round object created centrifugally – a complete object and a sustaining sensation. The conventional thrown pot has absolute uniform symmetry in the vertical dimension and therefore its shape can be taken in from one viewpoint by its silhouette.'[2]

But Britton wants forms that surprise the spectator from different viewpoints.

When she was at the Royal College of Art, Britton had several discussions with the potter Hans Coper, a part-time tutor in the Ceramics department. Coper impressed her, as he did other students at the Royal College, because he was an outsider, from Germany, making pots that had nothing to do with any aspect of English pottery. Moreover, although he used thrown forms, he created pots that Britton describes as 'having poise and symmetry and a more complex kind of form. Some Coper pots have dramatically different viewpoints – broad and monumental from the front, slender and elongated from the side. Thus there is not just one silhouette, there are many. They are pots that make new demands on the spectator.'[3]

Given her interest in asymmetry and a desire for a multiplicity of viewpoints it is, in retrospect, quite reasonable that Britton should have been drawn to making jugs, because their spouts and hands destroy the predictability of rotundity.

Jugs are naturally expressive objects: they have personality. Generally, a jug is an object of good cheer for dispensing milk and honey, or wine or beer. Putting a jug into the tragic mode amounts to miscasting. A jug offers a chance for irony or wit, and by turning a handle into a bustle or swelling the jug's chest

11

'Fish Jug', earthenware, 1976, h28cm. This is the nearest Britton has come to pushing the figurative potential of the jug form towards the 'Toby' jug category of literalness. Unlike the makers of Toby jugs or giftware ceramic animal sculptures, Britton has always, as she does here, abstracted some of the detail so that the piece as a whole becomes a decoration and not a model

and turning up its spout one can turn the thing into a pompous and swaggering character. And by emphasizing the fullness of the belly the jug can become a cheerful or blousy creature.

English potters enjoy jugs. The Toby jug, which emerged in Staffordshire in the eighteenth century and spread to the Continent, is an example. Toby jugs, which usually take the form of a man getting drunk, are, however, much more literal in their figuration than most of Britton's pots. Some of the oddest jugs to come out of England were made by the Martin brothers at the turn of this century: they made faintly monstrous and frequently manic jugs fashioned into grinning human faces; they are like characters in a story which you can script for yourself.

The fact is that the English feel comfortable with words and they like ornament that has a story to it. Rather poor pastiches of the original Toby jugs sell very well in modern giftware stores. The English preference for literal ornament helps to explain the popularity of Britton's jugs. She knows that her jugs were liked because they appeared to be 'about' something – they had the character of a bird or an animal or the personality of a human being. And, of course, the jugs looked functional, and this aspect of usefulness was a reassurance that these objects were sound at heart.

Britton did not often model her jugs into figures or animals, although there is one jug in the form of a fish which is about the closest she has come to making a Toby jug. What she preferred to do was to make jugs whose forms echoed the images that she was painting on the jugs. The jugs were designed for decoration in that being built from slabs (which were sometimes partially decorated before assembly), the jugs had a variety of viewpoints and flat planes that were ideal for decoration.

Most of the decoration in this period (1976-79) is childlike but not childish. At this time Alison Britton was using the British Museum as her resource. She was influenced by Early Greek, American Indian and Egyptian art. A characteristic of Egyptian painting, apart from its colour, is the fact that figures, animals, birds and objects were painted in profile and without a sense of perspective. Young children do the same thing. The Egyptians were not painting out of childlike ignorance, however, but from a convention that demanded of the artist that he include in a picture everything that is important about the figure or object depicted. Thus, if something had four legs, then four legs had to be shown irrespective of how it might look in real life, when from most viewpoints you would expect to see, say, three or even only two of the four legs.

Egyptian paintings, because of their rigid adherence to rules and conventions, and because they are often more like visual shopping lists or catalogues than descriptions of objects, yield a wealth of images that are ideal for patterns. They are flat and stylized and fall into natural rhythms of patterns and friezes.

The flattened images are rather like paper cutouts and they can be 'pushed' around the pot with ease and without regard for meaning. Britton took from Egyptian art a particular style, but none of its symbolism. The flexibility of this decoration is well demonstrated by *Triangular Jug* (1978), shown on page 14.

13

'Triangular Jug', earthenware, 1978, h32cm. The lines cutting up the surface were put in the clay before it was a jug, and the images arrived at in response to these arbitrary dividers. The Egyptian-style figures lend themselves to flat patterning – they can be pushed around a surface like cut-outs

Here we see the surface divided by green lines: these lines were put into the clay at the slab stage before the jug was finally assembled. The images of the figures were included as a response to these arbitrary dividers.

Because of the frieze-like quality of the decoration and the multi-faceted construction of the pots, turning a Britton jug around is like leafing through the pages of a book. And what warm 'books' they are! The colours of these jugs are pretty and merry. The warm, sandy background and the hot reds and greens make the surfaces sing and add to the jugs' conviviality.

The year after she made the jug in the form of a fish, Britton made a succession of jugs, among which there is one which is a minor tour de force as an ornament. It is a jug which Alison Britton disparages now as being too obvious: it is the *Stork Jug* (see page 41). Of course she is right; it is obvious but this is not a weakness. The jug is obvious in the sense that the illustration of the stork on the jug clearly reciprocates the form of the jug itself. Hence the shape of the bird's rump is complemented by the jug's handle, while the throat of the jug has exactly that muscular sinuousness that one would expect to find if one were to rub one's hand down a stork's neck – unlikely though such an experience may be. The beakiness of the spout reciprocates the beakiness of the bird. The line of the illustration and that presented by the profile of the form itself are the same in quality – tense, terse, and a bit spikey.

And so the 'obviousness' of this jug is all right; it is a cheerful, straightforward and potentially useful ornament. It has been executed with clarity; there is no fudging, no tricksiness and it remains fresh – as good ornament must.

Quentin Blake, Head of Illustration at the Royal College, said of the jugs: 'Alison Britton's works are essentially spontaneous – their wit is discovered, not applied; and feelings are able to flow into them. The work may begin as a jug, but it becomes a free-standing story, poem, situation.'[4] And Britton herself explained at the time: 'The ideas for drawings are not decided on before-hand but come in response to the form the piece has arrived at.'[5] Playfulness, free association and discovery are the key attributes to the creation of these works.

By 1978 the jugs had developed in two important ways. First, the interplay between the forms of the jugs and their decoration became more subtle. Second, the jugs themselves have much more sense of the three dimensions about them. Take, for example, the *Jug with Feathers* (1978) shown on page 38. We can see that it has depth and 'solidity' and elegance as well, while the faceting of the form entices you to turn the thing round. The lines where the planes meet have been sensitively exploited to give height to the pot, and our eyes are led up and down the pot rhythmically. It is a muscular jug: the planes are tensed up like sheets of muscle.

One of Britton's most sophisticated ornaments is *A Pair of Jugs* (1979), shown on page 44. Here it is as if two jugs, placed back to back, had merged, and what we see are the two sides and handles of each jug in relief on a perky double-beaked container. The 'jugs' have real beaks and pretend handles, and so there is a pretty play on reality and illusion and a neat theme for pattern-making. It is inventive without being ostentatious in its cleverness. She has taken the jug, half made it for real, but turned the other half into a fiction.

Lines and edges

Lines and edges, the abutting of planes, are dominant qualities in Britton's jugs. And although, as her work developed, she became more and more at home with making three-dimensional forms her jugs still had their roots in free-association drawing and the gesture of line. We already know that she does not like round forms, and in real life round forms betray very few outlines. In fact, lines and outlines, which Britton so emphatically uses in her pots, are less common in our everyday experiences than one thinks. Outlines are a device. This rather curious thought surprised Marion Milner, an English psychoanalyst who made a study of free drawing.[6] Milner wrote, 'I tried looking at the objects around me...When really looked at in relation to each other their outlines were not really clear and compact, as I had supposed them to be; they continually became lost.'

Milner suggests that the 'outline' represents the world of fact and that to cling to it is to protect oneself against the other world, the world of the imagination. Whether or not this holds for all of us, it proved to be an inspiration for Milner. She recounts that, having thought about the 'unreality' of outlines, she woke up one morning and saw two jugs on the table:

'Without any mental struggle I saw the edges in relation to each other, and how gaily they seemed almost to ripple now that they were freed from this grimly practical business of enclosing an object and keeping it in its place. Now it was easier to understand what painters meant by the phrase "freedom of line" because here, surely, was the reason for its opposite; that is, the emotional need to imprison objects rigidly within themselves.'

Marion Milner gave Alison Britton her first commission – for a tile surround to a fireplace. Milner is naturally interested in Britton's work, which in a sense is full of outlines so that within the confines of one pot one sees edges in relation to each other and these truly do ripple gaily. At the same time Britton is doing what a draughtsman does, establishing fixed viewpoints as 'facts', trying to determine how and from which points we should view any one of the pots. Her lines delineate fanciful objects. At the same time, lines and edges are an integral part of her strategy to make every part of the pot a component of the pattern; the lines both create unity and act as punctuation

Red-brown Yi hsing stoneware teapot, China, late Ming period. This is one of Britton's favourite historical pots. The articulated 'bamboo' handle and 'crustacean' spout are details echoed in some of Britton's jugs

17

marks. In one sense, these are three-dimensional drawings and their emphatic aspect is another clue to their popularity: there is no confusion over where to look.

The problem of popularity

It is doubtful if in 1979, the year when most of these jugs were assembled for the Crafts Council's exhibition, the work would have presented critics of pottery with any difficulties had they

been American. But there was at first hesitation among some of the older English experts because Britton was another of those 'young potters' who had broken completely with the orthodox Leach-style pot, whose rules and conventions were the criteria by which studio pots were judged. Indeed, as Victor Margrie, potter and former Director of the Crafts Council said, 'The leap from thrown pots for domestic use to slab-built jugs of rather doubtful function can present an impossible hurdle. A critical

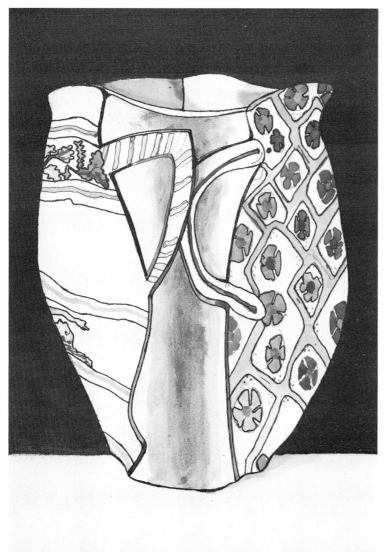

'A Pair of Jugs', earthenware, 1978, h29cm. A colour reproduction of this appears on p.44 but here in the drawing we can fully appreciate Britton's sense of pattern and her indebtedness to Egyptian painting, which combined both descriptive and abstract imagery into overall 'pattern' – see illustration drawn from the Egyptian room, British Museum, London

appreciation assiduously fed on a diet of reduced stoneware and the Oriental tradition can sometimes falter and a thoroughly unhelpful set of judgements be brought into play.'[7] Victor Margrie realized, and this took others a lot longer to learn, that there are a variety of valid approaches to making pots and that the criteria for judging them may not be interchangeable.

Yet once people were over their surprise, the jugs became popular. In a sense, Britton's work complements the decorative paintings by David Hockney: for while Hockney is a draughtsman and Britton is not, both caught the flavour of the period – it was a sort of dalliance with Californian flower power decoration made English and traditional by recourse to earlier decorative fashions including the European taste for mock Egyptian exotica. Throughout the 1970s Britton's pots evinced a well-mannered English decadence.

All kinds of people became fans of Britton's work and at the time they were made they were, and still are, alternative but very attractive ornaments. Their owners like the strong presence these jugs possess. Lord Eccles, the British patrician who set up the Crafts Council, said, 'the first of Alison's jugs which I bought, brawny and strong as Mohammed Ali, I put over the sink in my farm kitchen: the jug took dominion everywhere. Under its influence the pots and pans, the cooker and the furniture, became friends and sung in chorus.' We may blink at Eccles's excited geniality here, but he does establish a view of the Britton jug and its proper place, the home.

There is little doubt that Britton could have continued to make jugs for ever but she would have gone stale, and decorative art from a tired hand is always slight. So, there is little question about it: after the 1979 exhibition she had to move on. Her instinct was to loosen the connection with function but retain the discipline of working with the idea of the 'container'. She also determined to kill off some of the prettiness and keep her work sharp, not soft. It was time to come down from the mantelpiece.

ABSTRACTION

In Alison Britton's post-1980 pots there are few references to function other than the simple one of containing; the forms become architectural, even more asymmetrical and wilful. The decoration no longer recalls the symmetry of Egypt but instead strongly alludes to the work of abstract expressionist painters such as Jackson Pollock (1912-56). I do not want to over-emphasize the connection between Britton's decoration and Pollock's 'all-over' paintings, but the allusion to his work is there in Britton's abstract decoration and there are two reasons why this is unsurprising.

First of all, Britton belonged to that generation of British art students who were the first to get to know about American abstractionists; American painting generally made a huge impact on British art students throughout the 1960s. Secondly, there is a curious circularity about a modern English potter seeking out a gestural form of decoration. Sixty years ago we saw Bernard Leach and his followers trying to capture the fluency and intelligent spontaneity of the Oriental brushstroke and line. Here, with Britton, we see a similar interest in the informed gestural mark, but the association is with an art both more recent and closer in spirit to her own culture.

Pollock apparently could not draw. Robert Hughes, the Australian art critic, said of Pollock that his line 'had a laboured, blurting quality'.[8] But once Pollock began working with the canvas on the floor and began spattering skeins of paint from a height the line improved. He was able to use his whole body in swinging his paintstick around and that, plus gravity, gave his lines of paint a 'singular grace'. Pollock's innovation of the 'all-over' painting is regarded by Hughes as the most innovative development in pictorial space since the cubists. Pollock is the man who got furthest away from the idea of three-dimensional form: there are only lines and particles on a surface, no pictorial depth or content beyond an evocation of what Hughes calls that 'peculiarly American landscape experience'. Hughes believes that Pollock's best paintings were done between 1948 and 1950 and that they are decorative.

The question is whether such decoration is transferable. How well does its influence lend itself to the decoration of pots?

Pollock's work is virtually non-transferable because both the method of making it and the final impact of the work demands a single vast plane.

What is transferable and what Britton owes to Pollock is the principle that decoration can achieve a coherence without relying on geometry and without being predictable: what Pollock offers is the ultimate in asymmetrical non-narrative decoration. With the example of the abstract painters such as Pollock before her, Britton has clues on how to achieve the expressiveness of free line without the blurting. And 'blurting', a kind of deadness and clumsiness which stems from both the wrist and the brain, was the downfall of nearly all the English potters who have tried to capture the 'Oriental' line.

Finally, however, we must be clear that Britton's 'abstract' pots are not about painting; they are decorated pots.

Methods

How does Britton arrive at these pots? First, she takes her clay and rolls it out into a sheet and she then decorates this sheet with coloured slips (liquid clay). She does spatter and scatter the coloured slips and she works relatively quickly and freely. She uses a brush a lot and she thinks about the marks she is making in terms of the patterns that are created. The casual painting determines the shape and the outcome of the pot because it is the pattern which, cut into slabs, determines the composition of the container. Working on a sheet, then cutting it up into slabs, allows her to compose pots out of patterns that have been arrived at freely. Most of the sheet will be used but she can discard any parts that become chaotic or that she simply does not like.

Britton then decides on the basic shapes of the pot and cuts from the sheet of clay accordingly. These shaped slabs are joined together by crosshatching, or keying, the edges with a knife and painting water on them to form a slip. The two edges are then pressed hard together.

Her starting point for the basic shape depends on previous work: she does not jump from shape to shape arbitrarily but evolves and modifies ideas for forms. Outside influences can suggest modifications. In one group of pots made in 1984 she was struck by a painting by Fernand Léger, the French cubist painter (1881-1955), in which cones were stacked one on top of another. At the time she was already stacking cylinders asymmetrically, but there was a particular quality in the curvatures in Léger's cones which caught her eye.

The architecture of Britton's pots is quickly added to and rearranged as she cuts into planes and adds others: this is really prefabrication followed by carving and modelling.

The next stage involves further decoration with slips and the brush and then comes a first firing in the kiln. The coloured slips used in the first stages of the pots' creation are opaque, while the pigments that are used before the second firing are transparent. In addition to the decoration described, on many of Britton's recent pots there are interesting areas of rough, blistered texture and this has been built in at the first stage where she decorates the sheet of clay: she works in to some parts of her casual pattern small pieces of dry clay which provide that aged, buried quality of texture.

Risks

The risks Alison Britton is taking are clear: by loosening the form she loses the coherence and familiarity and discipline that the shape and function of the jug form provided for her. However, she could cheat because quite often the forms which the abstract pots take are reminiscent of jugs and by making, say, an overhang look more like a spout or by adding a large handle to a pot she could reintroduce the idea of function and so give the pot a familiarity. But Britton does not approve of such spurious familiarity. The point about the early jugs is that while they are essentially ornamental they were intended to be ornamental *jugs*; putting handles and spouts to the post-1980 pots would be a deceit.

Nonetheless, without the *need* to provide a spout here or a handle there, and without any hint of functional necessity about whether a form should be one way rather than another, there is the risk of arbitrariness. Moreover, Britton cannot be slotted into any conventional category and so what she has got to go on in judging whether a pot is good or not comes down to instinct and a sense of composition. These pots do not even abide by the convention that pots should *express* volume. The constituent parts of her work, the line, edge and slab, are those

of architecture, and, mostly, architecture surrounds space rather than expresses the volume within it. Britton's three-dimensional pots do not express volume.

Consider what she wants in her work and we see that we have a juggling act: she wants asymmetry, she wants a pot that offers several different viewpoints and she wants lively, non-geometrical or figurative patterns. She thus has to achieve a balance between the 'local' interference of an angular plane brightly coloured in an expressionist brushwork or with a

Granaries, Saskatchewan, Canada. Photograph taken by Britton when she visited North America in 1976. Although none of her later 'architectural' pots are representations of buildings either real or imagined there are clear echoes of influence and inspiration here in the forms and planes of these buildings and their relationship to one another

surface like a blistered paint-can, and the need for the viewer to be able to read the shape as a whole. If we cannot read the thing as a whole, if the local variations act too much like camouflage on a battleship, then our minds give up.

What she has done is create the pots in such a way that they present natural viewing points – they are meant to be looked at from different angles but not from every conceivable angle. By fixing dominant viewpoints she creates a structure and these viewpoints are mostly fixed by emphasizing vertical edges.

When she has the key viewpoints she wants, she can then pull up or push back the areas of 'local interest' in much the same way as a still life painter does. Horizontal lines, especially the line of the rim, are particularly useful as overall unifiers – they lead the eye around the pot and help to hold it together.

Expression and meaning

Alison Britton recently wrote what is in effect an explanation of how she regards her current work, although it was intended as a general comment on the British pottery world. 'I think that it is no longer useful to split the pottery world into two camps, the worthy and the decadent, the useful and the ornamental. There are no clear dividing lines to be drawn, and the same sort of criteria should be applied as far as possible to all sorts of pots, be they for daily use as a butter dish, occasional use as a vase, or, at the other extreme, imaginative use as an object of interest or enlightening beauty. It may be useful to make a comparison with prose and poetry. "Prose" objects are mainly active, concerned with use, and "poetic" objects are mainly contemplative, concerned with being looked at. For me the best objects are recognizable when I sense in looking at them a *frisson* from both aspects at once; both prose and poetry, purpose and commentary.'[9]

While I think we can agree with her illuminating analogy of prose and poetry, and the notion that the desirable pot is the one that has leanings towards both, I do not think it is reasonable to take the criteria that one uses to judge a thrown bowl and use it to judge, say, Britton's own work. There is a definite sense in which she and one or two other studio potters are out on a limb. True, in Britton's case she is close to home – what Lord Eccles said about a Britton jug taking dominion over the other objects in his kitchen applies equally to one of her latest ornaments placed in a living room. Her work enlivens and enriches a room with excitement and an operatic energy. Nonetheless, it is not possible to talk about Britton pots in conventional pottery terms – they are simply outside the criteria of conventional pots.

Yet ornament, which is what Britton makes, does not easily spring out of nowhere; it feeds off other sources and it is these sources that give ornament its 'meaning'. In the past ornament

'Scent bottle', Rhodes, 620 BC, is another of Britton's favourites. It is an interesting demonstration of how form and figuration can be simplified without any loss of personality – it is a combination of blunt draughtsmanship and solid modelling which takes the decorative away from the pretty into the expressive. This particular androgynous character appears to remind everyone of someone they know

has used symbols, images and devices that refer to aspects of the natural world, to myths, legends, to ideas that contribute to the corporate identity of a tribe or an institution or nation state. Successful ornament is usually the product of continuity: we like to be able to recognize something in an ornament or in decoration that we can understand. Sometimes we look for symbolism in our ornament.

You will not find overt symbolism in Britton's pots, but you will find all manner of echoes and allusions. Among the more obvious echoes in these pots are those of old houses and buildings. The larger planes of some of the pots bulge gently and with great strength like the aged walls of great houses; and the interiors of the pots, aided by the thick overhanging rims and lips, are like narrow streets in that the light is broken up and there is a great sense of an interior space in which one might wander. This is not to say that these pots are representative of such buildings – the echoes are too elusive in their allusions for that. Equally, the washed-out cobalt blues on their ochre surfaces suggest perhaps the sunlight and blue atmosphere of the Mediterranean just as with other pots the world they conjure is verdant and watery.

Britton's work is occasionally almost totemic: it alludes to the ritual and ceremonial functions that pots are used for in temples or for the rites of primitive tribes. Again, these are just suggestions, not assertions, but they are present in the pots that she has formed into groups. There is nothing ostentatious, anthropological or theoretical about these pots. Such echoes as they possess sit as lightly upon these pots as function does upon the jugs.

A DEVELOPING VIEW – A SHORT BIOGRAPHY OF ALISON BRITTON

Alison Britton was born in a North London suburb in 1948. Her father, James Britton, achieved fame as an expert on the teaching of English to children, her mother taught art, and one of Alison Britton's uncles, Donald Winnicott, was a psychoanalyst highly regarded for his writings on the nature of culture and creativity. In 1967 Britton went to Leeds College of Art to do a foundation year. She then spent three years at the Central School of Art and Design in London, followed by three years at the Royal College of Art, which she left in 1973.

In 1974, Britton was working on tiles and this was the period where she was beginning to discover not abstraction but figuration. This is what she wrote in 1974: 'My work went through a very gradual and difficult progress out of decoration into imagery. I was staggered at the freedom that came with the freedom to represent, rather than ornament. I found a new clarity in my ideas and that I had something to say at last – and a new emotional tie to what I was doing. I was very interested in the relationship of art to decoration, and the overlap that I feel exists there and which is probably of particular relevance to people working in the so-called crafts.'

This is interesting because in some respects Alison Britton has reversed her position – although this does not invalidate her work then or now, but rather reminds us of the variety of approaches that are possible. But it is a reminder of how much one is a child or a victim of the times. In the early 1970s the words 'ornament' and 'decoration' were at their most reviled. Fine art was moving off into areas far removed from the decorative camp in which rather a lot of abstractionists, especially English ones, had found themselves. Conceptual art with its esoteric ideas, white sheets of paper and empty rooms was one fashionable route but figuration was re-entering the theatre, if not yet actually on the stage. David Hockney consolidated his reputation in England and in the United States, while in England the longer-established painters, such as Francis Bacon and Lucian Freud, were receiving a wider and fairer critical appraisal.

It was not respectable to be associated with the crafts, which, in the United Kingdom in 1974, were entirely marginal. However, the embryonic Crafts Council, so important to the career of Alison Britton and many other craftsmen and craftswomen, was establishing itself. Crafts were forever receiving the qualifications 'so-called' by serious people working in craft media, because they felt they must distance themselves from the burden of whimsy and kitsch that crafts had come to be associated with. Looking back from 1985 it is clear that British professional craftsmen and craftswomen have much to be grateful for to bodies such as the Crafts Council which managed to separate the serious applied artist from the sheep-like makers of kitsch. The presence of so much bad work made in the name of 'craft' accounts for the extreme sensitivity among such people as the Royal College graduates in crafts. It also accounts for their strong desire to be identified with fine art. The expression 'artist-craftsman' was eagerly seized upon, even though by the end of the 1970s this had changed into an androgynous entity, the artist-craftsperson.

At this point, at the beginning of her professional career in 1974, Alison Britton was perhaps hypersensitive to the idea that what made craft 'art' was ideas. She was very specific about her ideas and wanted to rationalize the content of her work. In 1974 she wrote: 'The Survivor is my most important character, and appears in a lot of drawings as well as in two-and-a-half dimensions sitting on a cup and saucer. The figure first arrived in a drawing room of creatures, and gradually acquired significance the more I used him. He is part of a progression of bird/human figures, and seems to be the closest I have got to an archetype. I think he expresses a state of being, and aspects of humanity that I cherish. I use "he" in definition, though there is no firm gender; an isolated figure, ambiguous, quiet, unshowy, resilient. A "spectator" figure, calm, even nonchalant with folded arms, but entirely aware. The combination of ordinariness and specialness that I think magic consists of. He is shown on a tightrope, and "sitting on the edge" of things, his legs permanently bent for this. A figure highly conscious of his ground, he connects in my mind with some of Samuel Beckett's strange heroes.'

By 1983 such figurative content, literary allusions, and overly self-conscious reasoning and justification for making pots has gone. A statement provided that year for a catalogue gives a terser but less tense account: 'For a long time I liked to make jugs because of the simple restrictions that are imposed by lip and handle, and because of the stronger implications of usefulness. Now I am still concerned with vessels, but in a less specific way. As I stopped making jugs, my decoration changed from pictorial to abstract. With a developing sense of form, I was able to produce tougher, simpler shapes; and the imagery was out of place. My sources of inspiration and interest have also shifted from ancient and remote artefacts to include more modern things, like paintings and buildings. My work belongs on the "outer limits" of function – where function, or a reference to a possible function, is crucial but is just one ingredient in the final presence of the object, and not its only motivation.'

Understandably, she will not be drawn to answer the question, 'What next?'

1 *Five Furniture Pieces*, leaflet by Alison Britton for the British Crafts Centre, London 1985.
2 Article by Alison Britton for the catalogue published to accompany the British Council's *Contemporary British Ceramics* touring exhibition to Czechoslovakia 1984.
3 Ibid.
4 Crafts Council Exhibition Catalogue – *Alison Britton*, London 1979.
5 Ibid.
6 *On Not Being Able to Paint* by Marion Milner. (Heinemann Educational Books Ltd, 1981, paperback edition pp.15-17).
7 Crafts Council Exhibition Catalogue – *Alison Britton*, London 1979.
8 *The Shock Of The New* by Robert Hughes. Published by the British Broadcasting Corporation, 1981.
9 As 2.

Exhibitions and public collections
1976 Amalgam Gallery, London. (solo).
1977 Ceramics and Textiles. British Council touring exhibition to Middle East.
1978 Galerie Het Kapelhuis, Amersfoort, Holland. With Jacqui Poncelet.
'Five English Potters' at Princesshoff Museum, Leeuarden, Holland.
1979 'Jugs and Aprons'. Aberdeen Art Gallery and Museum. With Stephenie Bergman.
Prescote Gallery exhibition at Warwick House, London.
'Image and Idea'. British Council touring exhibition to Australia and New Zealand.
'The Work of Alison Britton' solo exhibition at Crafts Council Gallery, London.
1980 'British Ceramics Today'

touring America from Octagon Centre, Ames, Iowa.
'Ceramic Summer' at Sudbury Hall, Derbyshire.
'Prescote at Edinburgh' exhibition for Edinburgh Festival. Exhibition with Jacqui Poncelet at Galerie Het Kapelhuis, Amersfoort, Holland, continuing at Kruithuis Museum, Den Bosch, Holland.
1981 Solo exhibition at Prescote Gallery, Banbury, Oxon.
'British Ceramics and Textiles' at Scharpoord Cultural Centre, Knokke-Heist, Belgium.
Victoria and Albert Museum Craft Shop. Small solo exhibition.
1982 Galerie L, Hamburg, Germany. With Jacqui Poncelet.
'The Makers' Eye' exhibition, the Crafts Council. One of fourteen selectors.
Victoria and Albert Museum Craft Shop. Small solo exhibition.
Amalgam Gallery, London. With Jacqui Poncelet and Noela Hills.
Two group shows arranged by Henry Rothschild at the Scottish Gallery, Edinburgh, and in Eckenfode, Germany.
1983 'British Ceramics and Glass'. Convergence Gallery, New York. Part of 'Britain Salutes New York' Festival.
'Fifty-five Pots'. Orchard Gallery, Londonderry, N. Ireland.
Galerie Het Kapelhuis, Amersfoort, Holland. With Jacqui Poncelet and Walter Keeler.
Aspects Gallery, London. With Floris Van Den Broecke.
Oxford Gallery, Oxford. With Brian Illsley.
1984 Galerie L, Hamburg. International group exhibition.
Westminster Gallery, Boston, USA. With Jacqui Poncelet.
'Artist Potters Now'. Group show touring museums in Britain, from Oxford Museum.
Maya Behn Gallery, Zurich, Switzerland. British group exhibition.
'Black and White' exhibition at the British Crafts Centre, London.

Public Collections:
United Kingdom
Cecil Higgins Museum, Bedford; City Museums and Art Gallery, Birmingham; Cleveland Crafts Centre, Middlesborough; Crafts Council, London; East Midlands Museums Service; Hampshire County Museum Service; Leeds City Art Galleries (Temple Newsam); Museum and Art Galleries, Paisley; Leicestershire Museums; The Royal Scottish Museum, Edinburgh; Victoria and Albert Museum, London; and Ulster Museum, Belfast.

Abroad
Roymans van Reuningen Museum, Rotterdam, Holland; Kruithuis Museum, Den Bosch, Holland; Kunst und Gewerbe Museum, Hamburg, West Germany; The Living Museum, Kitchner, Ontario, Canada; The Melbourne Museum, Australia; The Princessehoff Museum, Leeuarden, Holland; The Stedelijk Museum, Amsterdam, Holland.

Writings
Elizabeth Fritsch catalogue for Leeds, 1978.
Accompanying notes for Chinese Mugs exhibition in ICA showcase, April 1979.
Introductory notes for Betty Woodman exhibition, Amalgam, March 1980.
Essay in The Makers' Eye' catalogue, Crafts Council, January 1982.
Contribution to Hans Coper valedictory issue *Crafts*, January 1982.
Review of 'Ceramics of the 20th Century', *Crafts*, January 1983.
'From Sevres to Krazy Kat', *Crafts*, March 1983.
Review of 'A Fresh Look at Earthenware', *Crafts*, November 1983.
Catalogue article for British Ceramics exhibition in Perth, Australia, February 1984.
British Crafts Centre leaflet '8 Ceramists', March 1984.
Catalogue article for Czechoslovakian touring exhibition of British Ceramics, British Council, written in March 1984 (published in Slovak).
Article on Hans Coper for *American Crafts*, April 1984.
Crafts Council leaflet on Stephenie Bergman, June 1984.
New Domestic pottery leaflet for Crafts Council, August 1984.
British Crafts Centre leaflet on Phil Sayer, September 1984.
British Crafts Centre leaflet for *Five Furniture Pieces* exhibition, January-February 1985.

Bibliography
Bennett, Ian, *British Twentieth Century Studio Ceramics* Christopher Wood Gallery, London 1980.
Casson, Michael, *The Craft of the Potter*, BBC, 1977.
Crafts Council catalogue, *The Work of Alison Britton*, John Houston and others for Alison Britton Exhibition, Crafts Council, 1979.
Dormer, Peter, *Alison Britton*, exhibition leaflet, Aspects Gallery, London, 1983.

THE WORK

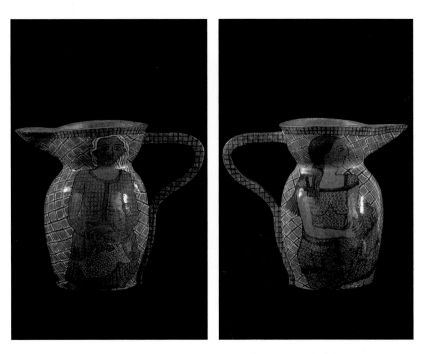

An early jug by Alison Britton, earthenware, 1976 h27cm

'Blue and White', earthenware, 1979 h27cm

'Jug', earthenware, 1978 h30cm. This example shows well how
Britton likes to transform an image into pattern and back again

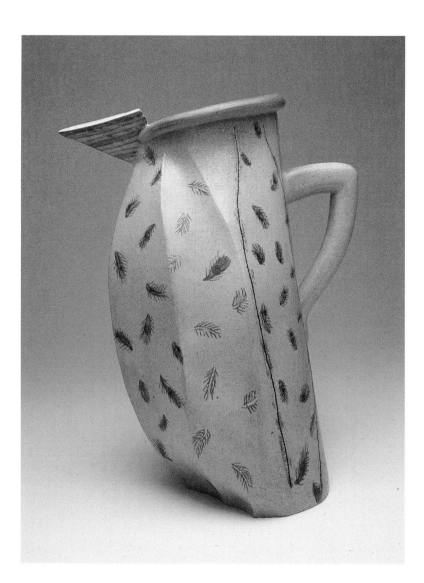

Above and previous two pages, 'Jug with Feathers', earthenware, 1978 h32cm. A very fine example of Britton's ability to capitalize on the expressive possibilities of the jug. Here the jug leans and swells like an elderly uncle about to give a younger relative some advice. The aspect of personality and human caricature is heightened by the frivolity of the decoration. This jug is thus an entertainment.

'Red Jug with Birds', earthenware, 1978 h32cm

'Stork Jug', earthenware, 1977 h30cm. A tour de force of
decoration – the form of the jug and the image complement one
another – the picture bird mirrors the jug bird and vice-versa.
The entire piece is alive with a rhythm of lines and outlines

'Big Striped Pot', stoneware, 1977 h35cm. In other circumstances
the pretty frieze of leaves around the rim would have been fey,
but the robustness of the forms and the strong graphic decoration
gain from the light relief of the frieze

'Red Bird Jug', red earthenware, 1977 h31cm.
'Little Jug with Feet', red earthenware, 1977 h24cm.

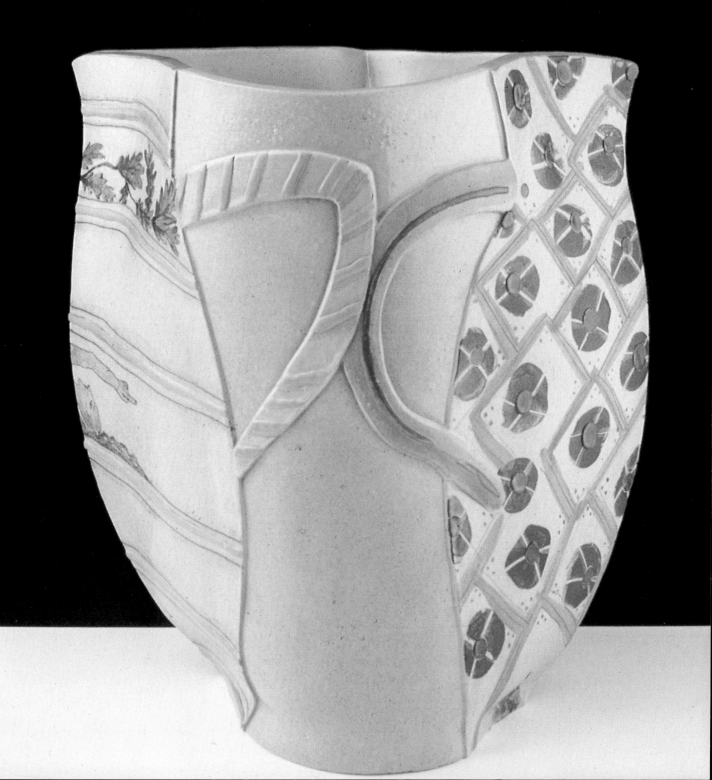

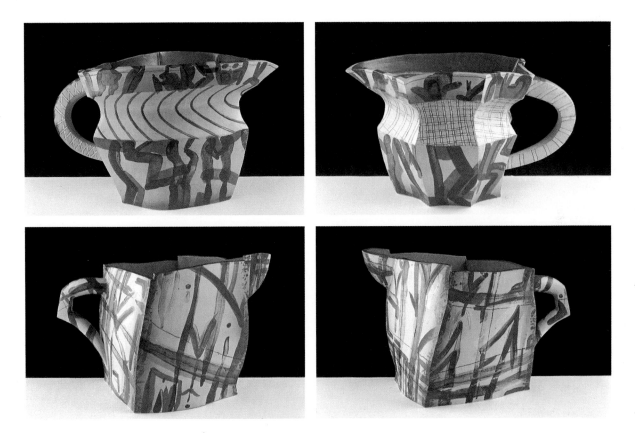

*Top left and right, 'Two Faced Jug', earthenware, 1979 h30cm
Bottom left and right, 'Squat Square Jug', earthenware,
1979 h26cm*

*'A Pair of Jugs', earthenware, 1979 h29cm. Two jugs back into
each other and a pretty play between pattern and form is the result*

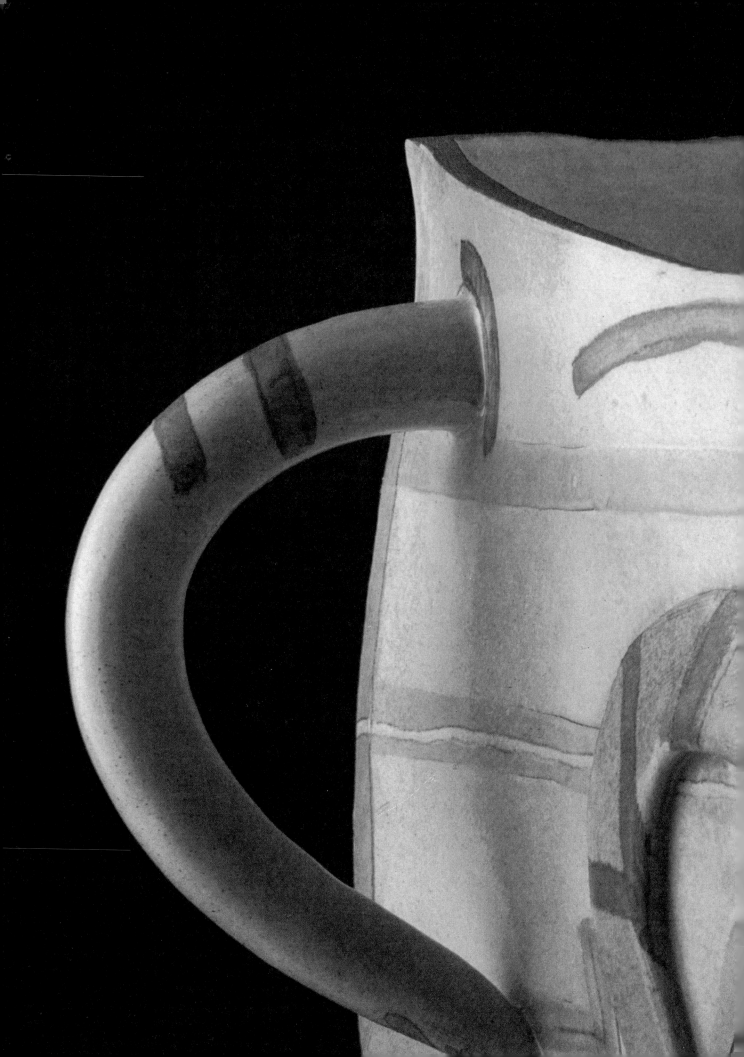

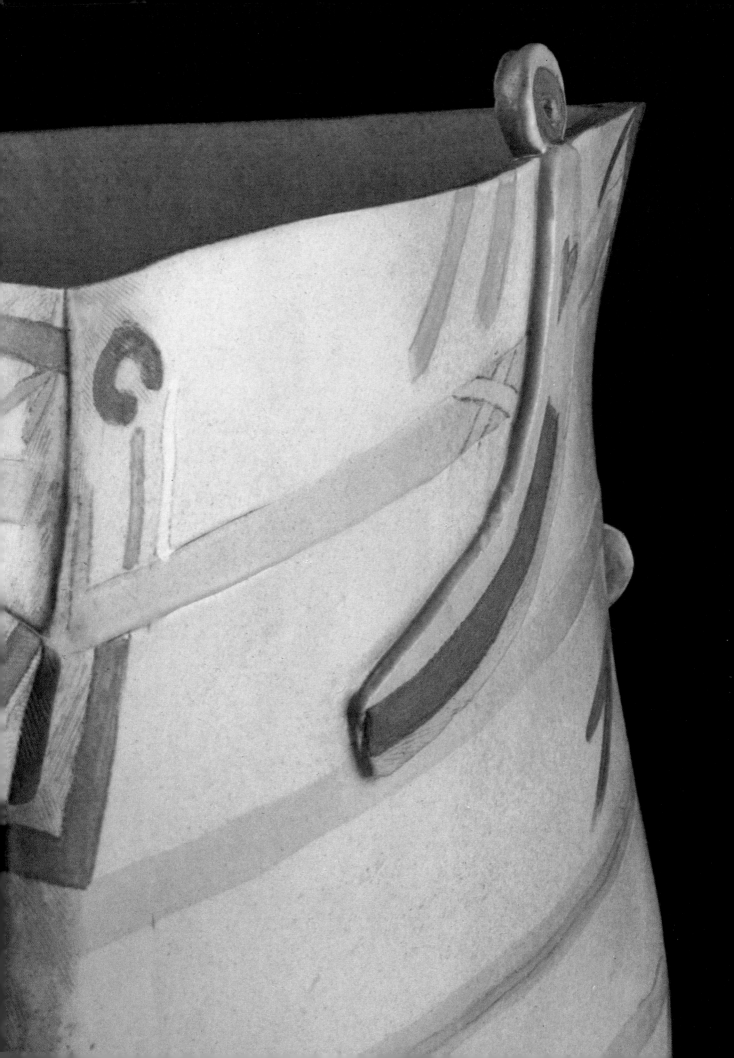

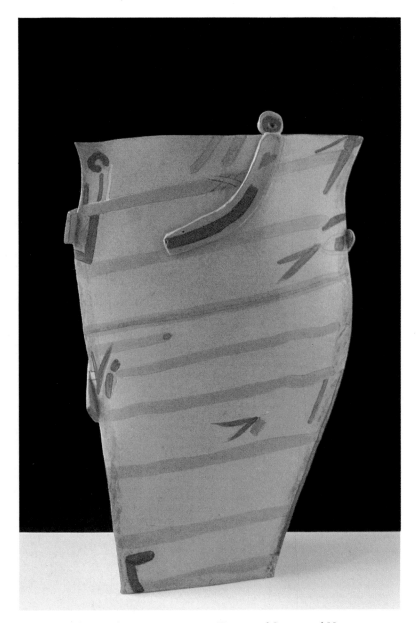

*Above and previous two pages, 'Straps and Stripes and Hearts
and Flowers', earthenware, 1979 h37cm. The 'jug' aspect here is
clearly just a vehicle – the echo of function and utility simply
provides a meaning and structure for this light-hearted ornament.
The handle, for example, is placed for compositional and not
practical reasons*

'Pair of Jugs', earthenware, 1978 h26cm and 32cm

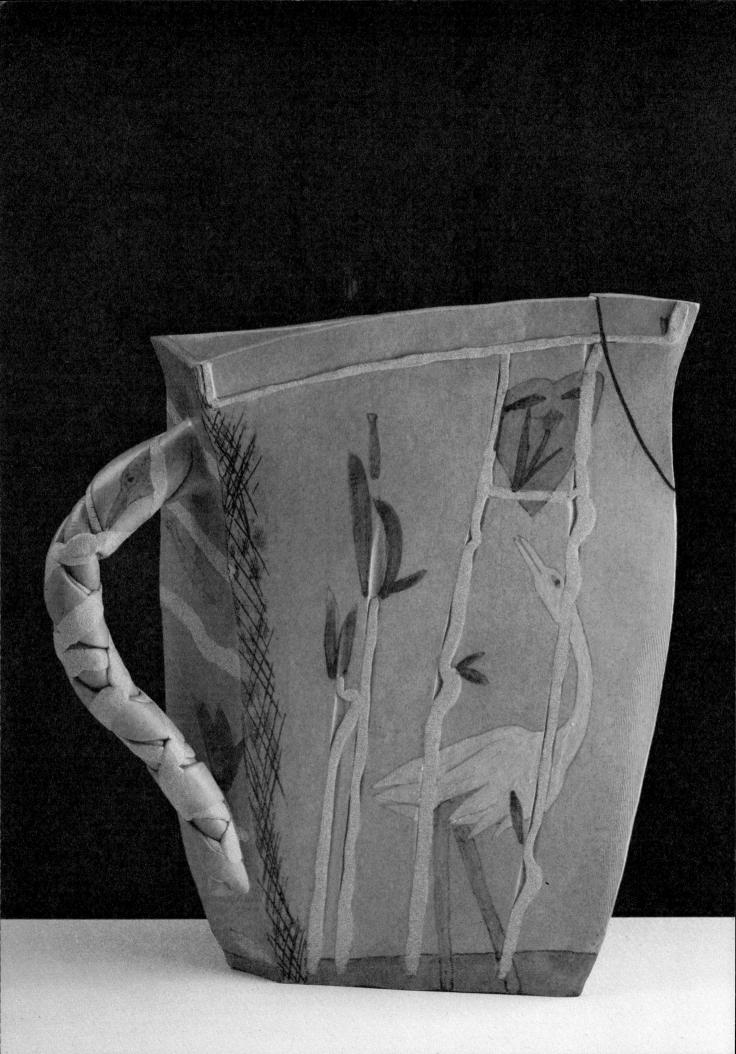

Top left, 'Goldfish Jug', earthenware, 1979 h36cm
The congruence of the form's rhythm and the floating decoration
bending with the current of the water is delightful – the whole jug
is flexing like a reed. The flashes of white on the spout act like
highlights on water
Top and bottom right, 'Flat Fronted Jug', earthenware,
1978 h30cm
Bottom left, 'Water Jug', earthenware, 1979 h30cm

'Caged Stork', earthenware, 1979 h29cm

Left, 'Round Bottomed Jar', earthenware, 1981 h26cm
Right, 'Small Green and Magenta Squares', earthenware,
1981 h28cm

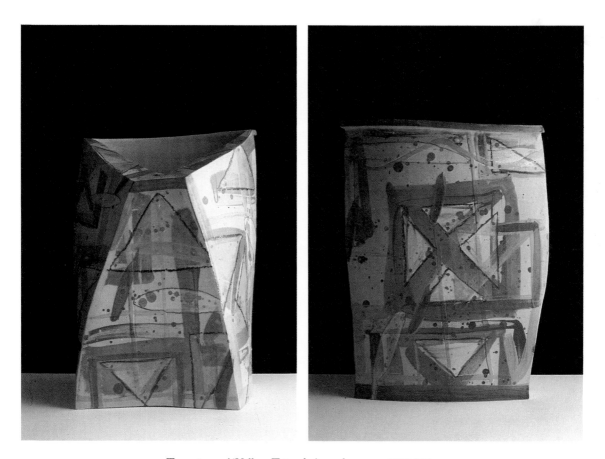

Two views of 'Yellow Triangles', earthenware, 1981 h28cm
This pot invites comparison with the work of Clarice Cliff.
Clarice Cliff was a decorative potter whose designs are
unconventional and wayward—gaudy, gawky, abstract and
dramatic. She, like Britton, was a decorator who suppressed
prettiness

'Stevie's Cup', earthenware, 1979 h14cm. Alison Britton
comments, 'This is coiled rather than slab-built. The softer inside
shape made by coiling seemed to demand attention, as in Palissy
sauce boats which I like very much. But having painted this, I
prefer the piece in profile'

'Pot with Shoals', earthenware, 1978 h30cm

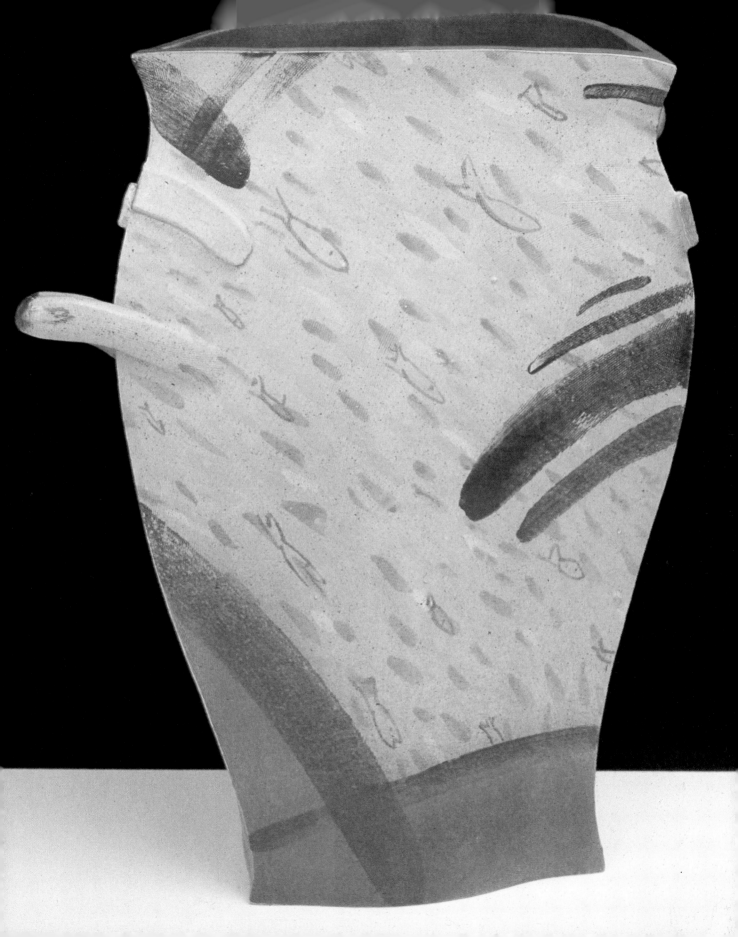

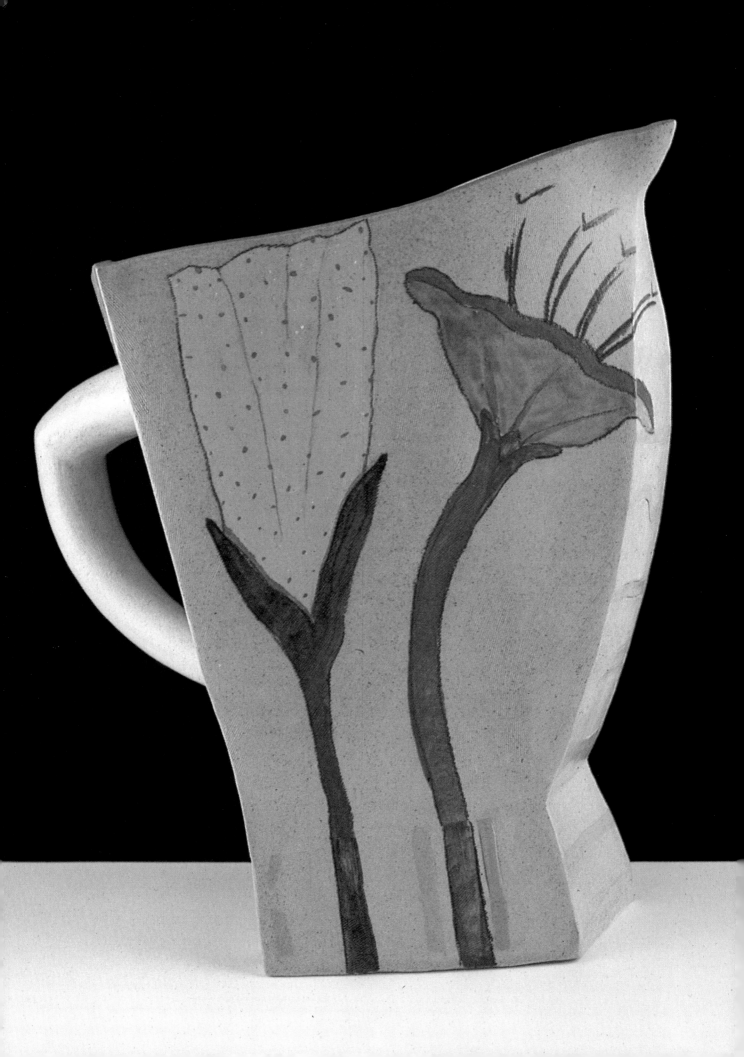

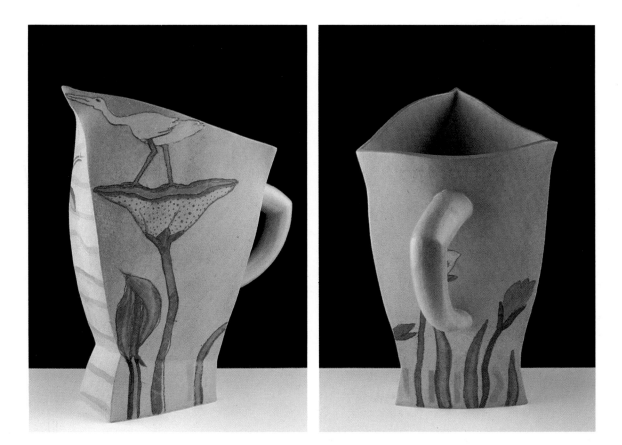

Three views of 'Jug with Stalk', earthenware, 1979 h26cm
The images unfold like a book as you turn the pot around –
Britton's intention has been to get away from
two-dimensional ornament

'Set of Tulip Jugs', earthenware,
1978 h29, 24cm, 32cm

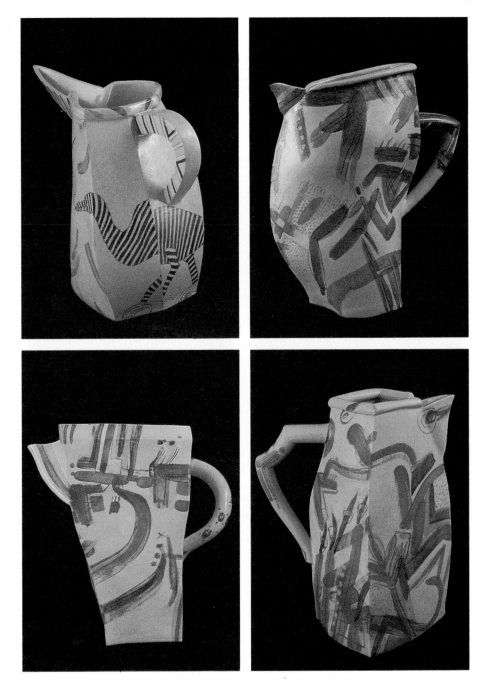

Top left, 'Jug with Striped Bird', earthenware, 1978 h29cm
Top right, 'Pink, Green and Brown Jug', earthenware, 1978 h33cm
Bottom right, 'Small Square Jug', earthenware, 1978 h27cm

'Big Square Jug', earthenware, 1978 h36cm, see also bottom left

'Tall Triangle and Square Bowl', earthenware, 1983 h32cm, 26cm

'Big Green Pot', earthenware, 1982 h32cm. What Britton has
been searching for since moving on from her decorative jugs is
ornament that is tough, modern and without literary or figurative
allusions. She has sought to dampen down the prettiness.
   This piece owes its decoration to the influence of abstract
expressionist painters whose work is a part of every contemporary
artist and applied artist's knowledge. In a sense her adoption of
the expressionist gesture is a continuation of the British potters'
fascination with the Oriental brush stroke which Bernard Leach
and his followers used for the decoration of their pots. This pot is
architectural in its construction, it has little to do with the
expression of volume but it is determinedly three-dimensional –
like a ranging, idiosyncratic building. It is not, however, a
representation of a building – or of anything else

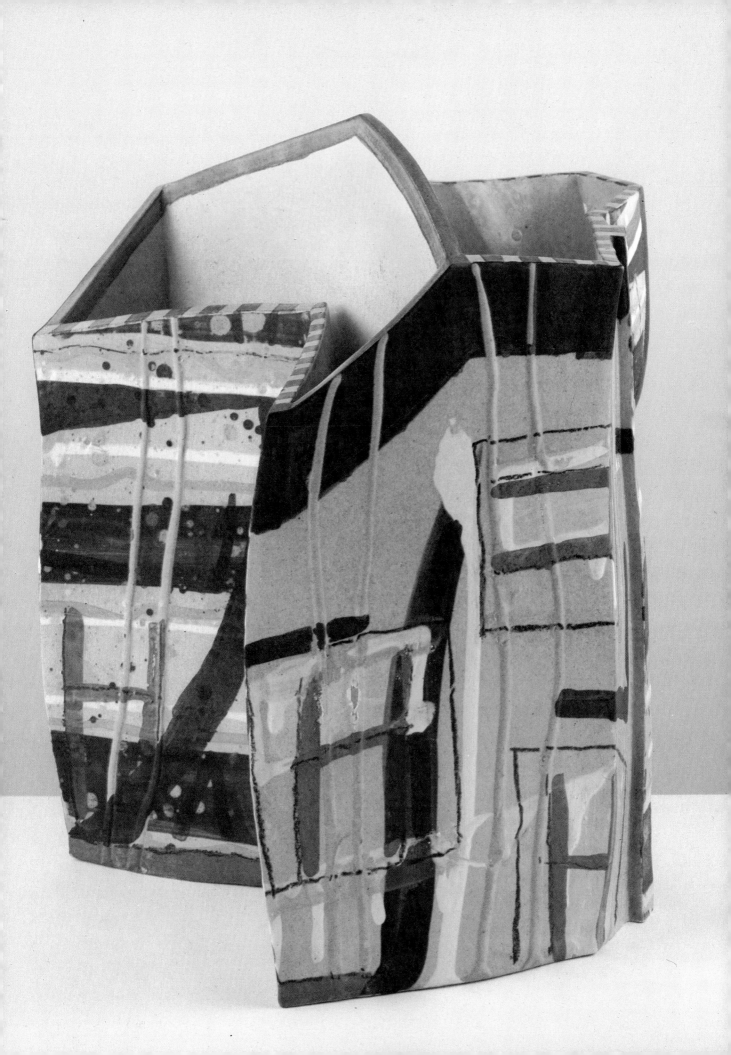

'Big Green Jug', earthenware, 1979 h31cm, and facing page

'Double Based Jug', earthenware, 1979 h30cm, and facing page, left

Right, 'Three Hearts', earthenware, 1979 h27cm

'Green Squares', earthenware, 1982 h29cm. The two views of
this bold, stately pot reveal Britton's technique of building in
dominant viewpoints to which one is naturally attracted. This is important because although
it is exciting to have objects which present an ever-changing aspect as they are turned
round, they must also have an overall coherence.
One needs to be able to read
both the form and the pattern. If the pattern begins camouflaging
the form like a battleship then the pot would become visually confusing and tiresome to look at.
Composition is just as important in ornament as it is in every area of design or visual art
Bottom left and right, 'Blue and Black Triangle', earthenware, 1982 h28cm

'Big Yellow Pot' (also cover illustration), earthenware, 1981 h33cm
The interiors of her pots are as important as the exteriors – the
overhangs along the rim break up the light and create mysterious
shadows. The outside texture is created by rubbing in dried clay
particles into the moist clay sheet before firing

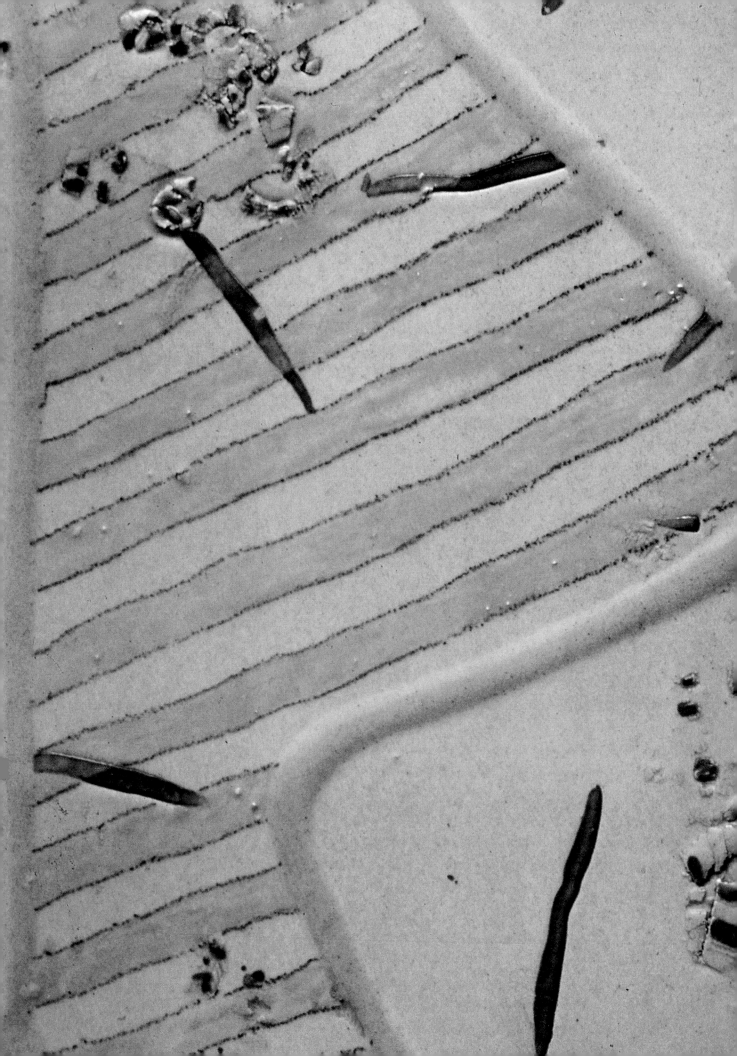

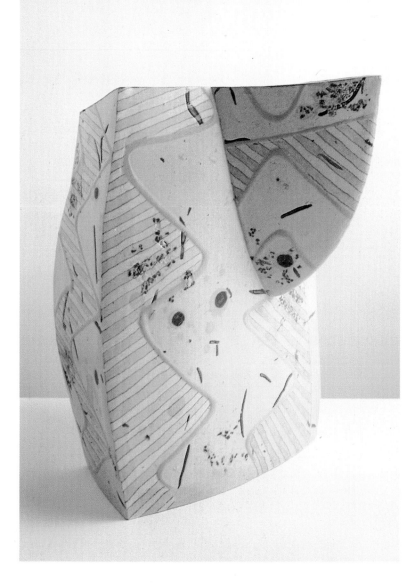

*Above and previous two pages, 'Green Zig Zags with Spout',
earthenware, 1981 h30cm*

*'Intercepted Pot', earthenware, 1982 h28cm. An example from
Britton of the pot as three-dimensional drawing. In effect this pot
is a striking reworking of 'A Pair of Jugs', p.44 – two pots put
together as one but still retaining their 'separateness'*

Two views of 'Blue and Black', earthenware, 1981 h27cm

'Black and Blue', earthenware, 1982 h26cm

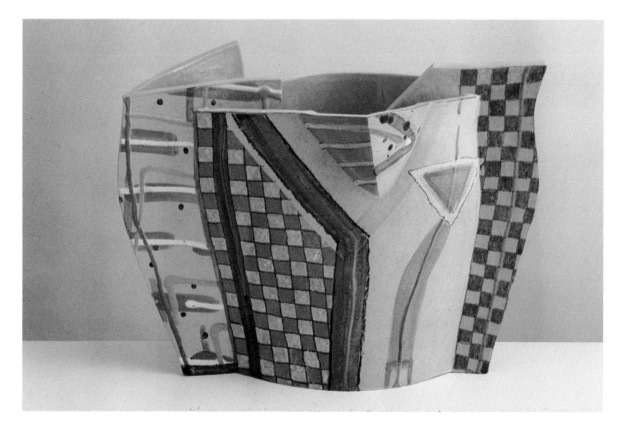

'Blue and White', earthenware, 1982 h28cm

'Pair with Black Lines', earthenware, 1981 h24cm, 25cm
Here and on the facing page we see that although asymmetry is a
characteristic of Britton's work she frequently uses the device of
pairing images or pairs of pots to provide an overall scaffolding
within which the detail of decoration, line and form can play

Top, 'Spotted Pot', earthenware, 1982 h26cm
Bottom, 'Yellow Zig-Zag Pot', earthenware, 1982 h30cm

'Grey Edges and Fish', earthenware, 1982 h28cm

'Three Pieces Together',
earthenware, 1982 h27cm, 22cm, 27cm

'Black and Blue', earthenware, 1983 h29cm, and facing page

Preceding spread: Three pieces together, earthenware, 1982 h27, 22, 27cm

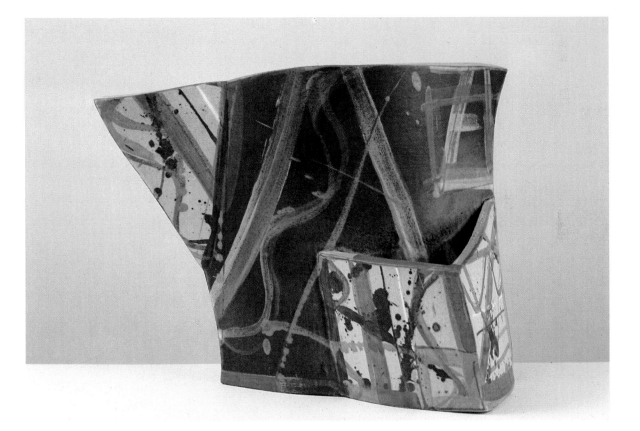

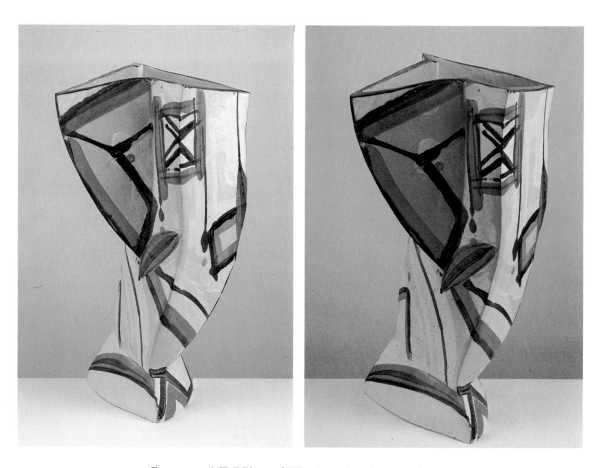

Four views of 'Tall Blue and White', earthenware, 1983 h36cm
This could function as a vase but it is really an example of the
vessel as an excuse for ornament. It is intended as a lively,
dominating piece of decoration rather than as a sculpture with all
the metaphorical implications which that would entail. Britton has
an intense dislike of whimsy. She has sought out the decorative

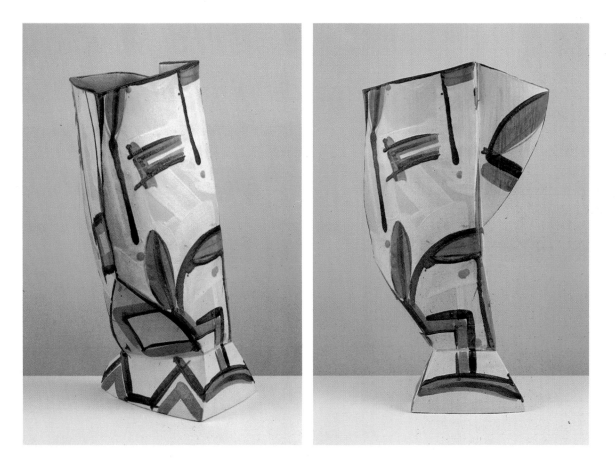

but declined the pretty, and she has prevented the abstraction
from becoming arbitrary by keeping the vessel firmly as a theme,
as her core structure. The vessel has provided the ornamentalist
potter with a convenient peg or theme in much the same way as
the human figure has provided a theme and a peg
for the painter or sculptor

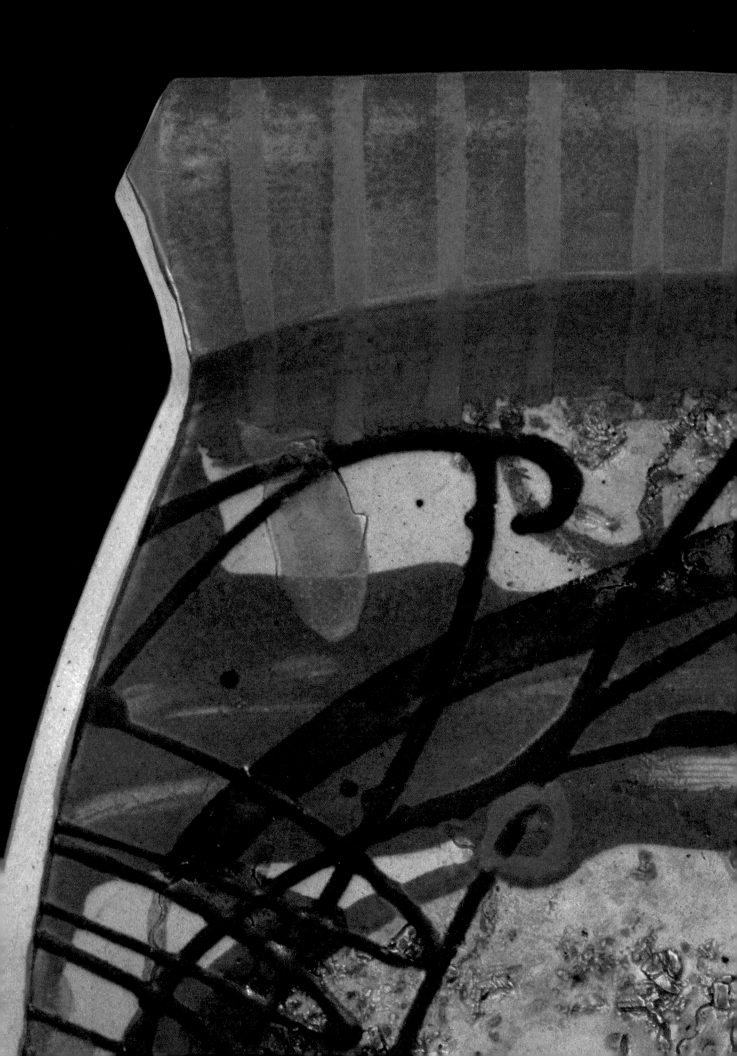

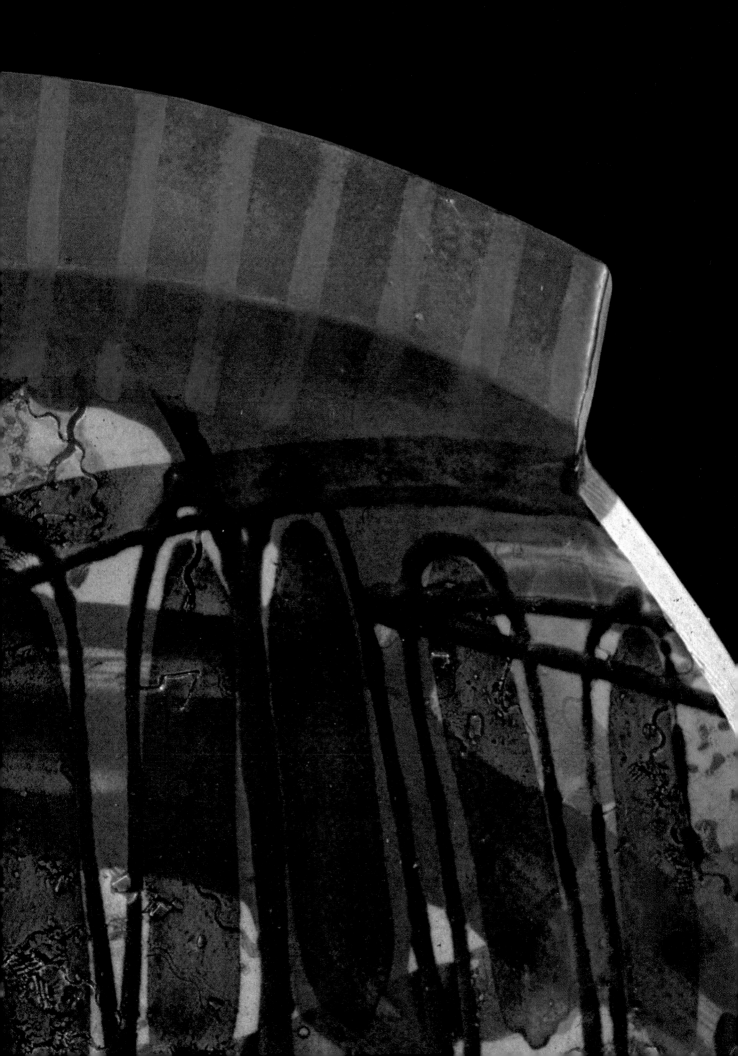

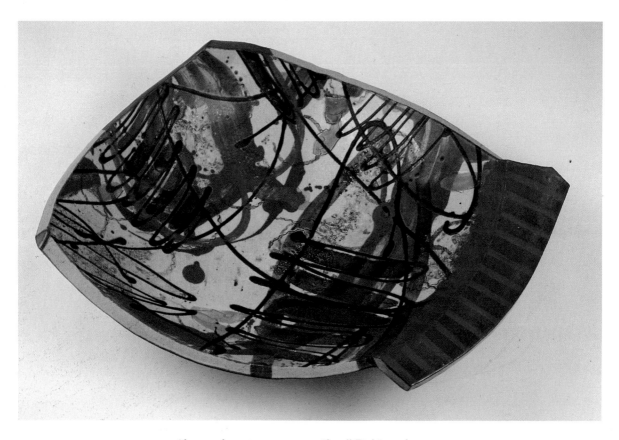

*Above and previous two pages, 'Small Dish', earthenware,
1983 w33cm*

*'Jug', earthenware, 1982 h35cm. Jackson Pollock et al have been
treated by several decorative artists as a natural
resource for loose pattern*

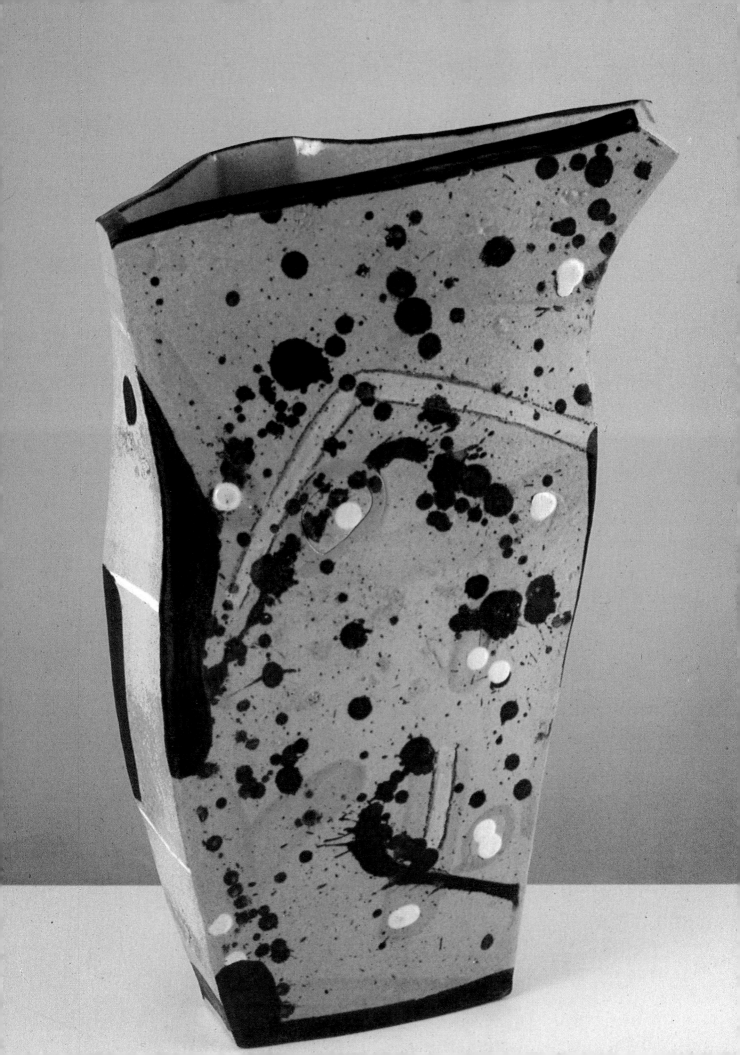

Left and right, 'Grey Eyes', earthenware,
1982 h34cm

Left and right, 'Maroon and Grey Angles', earthenware,
1982 h34cm

Left, 'Pot on Base', earthenware, 1983 h30cm
Right, 'Green and Red Double Pot', earthenware, 1983 h33cm

'Green and Beige and Turquoise Pot', earthenware, 1983 h33cm

Left, 'Beige Pot with Green Triangles', earthenware, 1984 h39cm
Right, 'Beige and Pink', earthenware, 1984 h39cm
Although these works do not have a content – there is no point in asking
what they 'mean' – they nonetheless are rich in allusions.
The odd, cockeyed 'architecture' and the encrusted surfaces suggest
something very old or connected with the sea, with landscape, with growth.
This echoing or suggestiveness is what good pottery often contains – it can
provide a starting point for private musings and associations which is
what makes pottery ornament a private and domestic art

'Beige Striped Pot with Blue Spirals', earthenware, 1984 h39cm

'Intercepted Pot', earthenware, 1982 h28cm,
see page 73

INDEX